GETTING TO KNOW THE WORLD'S GREATEST ARTISTS

G R A N T
WOOD

WRITTEN AND ILLUSTRATED BY MIKE VENEZIA

CONSULTANT MEG MOSS

CHILDRENS PRESS®
CHICAGO

JB
Wood

For Rhea Sprecher.
Thanks for your help and inspiration.

Cover: *American Gothic*, by Grant Wood. 1930. Oil on beaver board,
29¹/₄ x 24¹/₂ inches. The Art Institute of Chicago, Friends of American Art
Collection. Photograph © 1994 The Art Institute of Chicago. All Rights Reserved.

Project Editor: Shari Joffe
Design: PCI Design Group, San Antonio, Texas
Photo Research: Jan Izzo

Library of Congress Cataloging–in–Publication Data

Venezia, Mike.
    Grant Wood / written and illustrated by Mike Venezia.
    p.   cm. -- (Getting to know the world's greatest artists)
    Summary: Relates the artistic career of the Iowan who painted
    people, life, and customs of the American Midwest and whose
    style became known as Regionalism.

    ISBN 0-516-02284-9 (lib. bdg.)—ISBN 0-516-42284-7 (pbk.)
    1. Wood, Grant, 1891-1942--Juvenile literature.
    2. Artists--United States--Biography--Juvenile literature.
    [1. Wood, Grant, 1891-1942. 2. Artists.]
    I. Title.   II. Series: Venezia, Mike.
    Getting to know the world's greatest artists.
    N6537. W66V46 1995
    759 .13--dc20
    [B]   95-7023
                         CIP
                         AC

Copyright 1995 by Mike Venezia.
All rights reserved. Published simultaneously in Canada.
Printed in the United States of America.
   4 5 6 7 8 9 10 R 04 03 02 01 00 99

Photograph of Grant Wood with *Arbor Day*, 1932. Photograph by John W. Barry.
Cedar Rapids Museum of Art Archives, Gift of John B.Turner II in memory of
Happy Young Turner. © Cedar Rapids Museum of Art.

Grant Wood was born on a farm
near the small town of Anamosa,
Iowa, in 1891. By painting simple
scenes of the land and people he
knew best, he helped create an
important, all-American style of art.

Grant Wood's paintings
show the love he had for the
people and customs of the
midwestern United States.

Dinner for Threshers, by Grant Wood.
1934. Oil on hardboard, 20 x 80 inches.
The Fine Arts Museums of San Francisco,
Gift of Mr. and Mrs. John D. Rockefeller III,
1979.7.105.

Detail of *Dinner for Threshers.*

Grant particularly loved the farmland of Iowa. While growing up, he enjoyed feeling the soft, warm soil between his toes as he walked barefoot through the fields.

In his painting *Young Corn*, it seems like the round, friendly hills are protecting the farmer and his children while they work in their fields.

Young Corn, by Grant Wood. 1931.
Oil on masonite panel, 24 x 29 7/8 inches.
Cedar Rapids, Iowa, Community School District.

GRANT WOOD·1931

Stone City, Iowa, by Grant Wood. 1930. Oil on wood panel, 30 1/4 x 40 inches. Joslyn Art Museum, Omaha, Nebraska.

During Grant Wood's time, other artists, like John Steuart Curry and Thomas Hart Benton, also began painting pictures of activities in the midwestern regions where they lived. This was one reason their style of art became known as Regionalism.

Tornado Over Kansas, by John Steuart Curry. 1929. Oil on canvas, 46 1/2 x 60 3/8 inches. Muskegon Museum of Art, Muskegon, Michigan, Hackley Picture Fund.

Boomtown, by Thomas Hart Benton. 1928. Oil on canvas, 45 x 54 inches. Memorial Art Gallery of the University of Rochester, Marion Stratton Gould Fund.

9

Grant Wood showed an interest in
art at a very early age. He often drew
pictures with burnt sticks his mother
gave him from her stove. Even
though Grant drew pictures every

chance he got, everyone thought
he'd grow up to be a farmer, like his
father. Grant seemed to enjoy his
farm chores, and had his own goats,
chickens, ducks, and turkeys.

When Grant was ten years old, a very sad thing happened to him. His father died, and his mother found that it was too difficult to keep the farm running. She decided to move her family to the nearby city of Cedar Rapids. It was a hard move for Grant. He missed his farm pets, and felt out of place in the new city school. Some kids even made fun of him.

Societies, by Grant Wood. 1908. Ink and wash on paper, 6 1/4 x 4 1/16 inches. © Cedar Rapids Museum of Art, Art Museum Purchase.

SOCIETIES

Because of his good sense of humor and his talent for drawing, things eventually got better for Grant. In high school, he made friends, and was always busy working on projects, like designing scenery for school plays and drawing pictures for the school paper and yearbook.

After he graduated, in 1910, Grant did a lot of different things. He took art classes, taught art, made jewelry, learned carpentry, decorated people's houses, and cared for his mother and his sister, Nan.

He loved gadgets and making
things, and he worked slowly
and carefully at all his crafts.

He was even able to use his
artistic talent when he joined the
army, during World War I. His
job was to paint camouflage on
tanks and cannons.

The Place du Havre, Paris, by Camille Pissarro. 1893. Oil on canvas,
23 ³/5 x 28 ⁹/10 inches. The Art Institute of Chicago. Mr. and Mrs. Potter Palmer
Collection. Photograph © 1994, The Art Institute of Chicago. All Rights Reserved.

During this time, American
art students were often encouraged
to study and paint in the style
of the great 19th-century French
Impressionist artists. In 1920,

Avenue of Chestnuts, by Grant Wood. 1920. Oil on composition board, 13 x 15 inches.
© Cedar Rapids Museum of Art, Gift of Happy Young and John B. Turner II.

Grant decided to travel to Europe
to study artists like Pierre Bonnard,
Alfred Sisley, and Camille Pissarro.
It's easy to see the influence these
Impressionist artists had on him.

Grant thought his paintings were getting pretty good, but felt something important was missing from them. He wanted to find a style that better fit his careful way of working.

On one trip to Germany, Grant saw the works of some old master painters of the 15th century. He became interested in the way artists like Albrecht Dürer and Hans Memling painted everyday people clearly and simply, using smooth, carefully blended brush strokes. This was much different from the Impressionists, who created an "impression" of a scene by putting their paint on more thickly, with quick brush strokes.

Portrait of a Man in a Red Hat, by Hans Memling. © 1467-70.Oil on oak panel, 16 2/5 x 12 inches. Stadelsches Kunstinstitut, Frankfurt, Germany. Photograph Ursula Edelmann /ARTOTHEK.

Grant also liked the way the old masters took time to paint the background detail and decorative clothing of their day.

Woman with Plants,
by Grant Wood.
1929. Oil on
upsom board,
20 1/2 x 17 7/8
inches. © Cedar
Rapids Museum
of Art, Art
Association
Purchase.

It was soon after his trip to
Germany that Grant found a
way to paint that was all his own.
He decided to paint the subjects
he knew and loved, using some
of the simple ideas of the old
European masters. Grant realized

that scenes of the people and places he knew while growing up were as beautiful and important as anything he had seen in Europe.

In *Woman with Plants*, Grant painted his mother as a strong and loving frontier woman. He placed her in a farm landscape, and paid special attention to the decorative stitching on her dress, the cameo around her neck, the potted plant, and other details that were important to her.

People all over Iowa were proud of Grant's portrait of his mother. It was one of the first paintings about the Midwest that seemed like it was done by someone who really knew and understood the people there. Grant kept working in his new style and soon painted his most famous picture, *American Gothic*.

One day, while Grant was looking for something interesting to paint, he discovered a farmhouse with an unusual window. The arch-shaped window was based on a style of European architecture from the Middle Ages called Gothic architecture. Grant liked the contrast of a European window on an American farmhouse.

After he made sketches of the house, Grant looked for just the right people to go with it. He thought his family dentist and his own sister, Nan, would be perfect for the farmer and his daughter.

American Gothic, by Grant Wood. 1930.
Oil on beaver board, 29 1/4 x 24 1/2 inches.
The Art Institute of Chicago. Friends of American
Art Collection. Photograph © 1994 The Art
Institute of Chicago. All Rights Reserved

Grant entered *American Gothic* in a big show at the Art Institute of Chicago, and won the third-place prize. People all over America loved the newspaper pictures they saw of it.

Person Throwing a Stone at a Bird, by Joan Miro. Oil on canvas, 29 x 36 1/4 inches. The Museum of Modern Art, New York. Photograph © 1995 The Museum of Modern Art, New York. Purchase.

Painting with Green Center, by Wassily Kandinsky. 1913. Oil on canvas, 43 1/5 x 47 2/5 inches. The Art Institute of Chicago, Arthur Jerome Eddy Memorial Collection. Photograph © The Art Institute of Chicago. All Rights Reserved.

Soon, Grant's paintings started to become very popular. One reason for this was that many people felt Grant's art was easier to understand

than a lot of the new modern
art being done at the time by
artists like Wassily Kandinsky
and Joan Miro.

Another reason Grant's paintings became so popular was that they came along during a rough time in history known as the Great Depression. The depression caused many people to lose their jobs and savings. It made people feel better to look at Grant Wood's paintings of beautiful farm lands and proud, hard-working families who helped make America great.

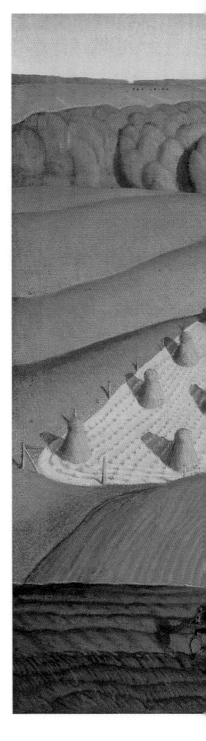

Fall Plowing, by Grant Wood. 1931.
Oil on canvas, 30 x 40 3/4 inches.
Courtesy Deere & Company, Moline, Illinois.

Midnight Ride of Paul Revere, by Grant Wood. 1931.
Oil on composition board, 30 x 40 inches. The Metropolitan
Museum of Art, Arthur Hoppock Hearn Fund, 1950. (50.117).
© 1988 The Metropolitan Museum of Art.

Grant also painted pictures of famous American legends. While growing up, he had loved the stories he heard about George Washington and Paul Revere.

In *Midnight Ride of Paul Revere,* Grant showed the story as he imagined it as a child. He painted broccoli-shaped trees and toylike houses. The roads go off into the background and seem to glow in the dark. Grant gave his painting an almost fairytale look. Paul Revere's horse even looks more like a wooden rocking horse than a real horse!

Grant was very clever and was an excellent craftsman. He not only painted, but also made prints, drawings, sculptures, and book illustrations. Grant also started an art colony, and designed one of the largest stained-glass windows ever made.

Veteran's Memorial Building Window, by Grant Wood. 1929. Stained glass. Veteran's Memorial Commission, City of Cedar Rapids, Iowa.

Parson Weems' Fable, by Grant Wood. 1939. Oil on canvas, 38 3/8 x 50 1/8 inches. Amon Carter Museum, Fort Worth, Texas.

Grant Wood died in 1942. It had taken him many years to find a way to paint that he felt was special enough to call his own.

After searching the art centers of Europe, Grant had finally realized that the best place to create art was right in his own backyard. To Grant Wood, there really was no place like home!

Spring in Town, by Grant Wood. 1941. Oil on panel, 26 x 24 1/2 inches. Courtesy Sheldon Swope Art Museum, Terre Haute, Indiana.

When Grant Wood painted *American Gothic*, he was just having fun showing the kind of people he had known all his life. He was surprised when it got so much attention. Everyone seemed to have an

Nan Wood Graham and Dr. B.H. McKeeby next to American Gothic, 1942, at the Art Institute of Chicago. Cedar Rapids Museum of Art Archives, Gift of John B. Turner II in memory of Happy Young Turner. © Cedar Rapids Museum of Art.

opinion about it. Some people thought Grant was making fun of farmers, while others thought he was honoring them. One reason *American Gothic* has become so popular is that very often, people see something in it that reminds them of themselves.

The works of art in this book came from the places listed below:
Amon Carter Museum, Fort Worth, Texas
The Art Institute of Chicago, Chicago, Illionois
Cedar Rapids Musem of Art, Cedar Rapids, Iowa
Community School District, Cedar Rapids, Iowa
Deere & Company, Moline, Illinois
The Fine Arts Museums of San Francisco, San Francisco, California
Joslyn Art Museum, Omaha, Nebraska
Memorial Art Gallery of the University of Rochester, Rochester, New York
The Metropolitan Museum of Art, New York, New York
The Museum of Modern Art, New York, New York
The Muskegon Museum of Art, Muskegon, Michigan
Sheldon Swope Art Museum, Terre Haute, Indiana
Stadelsches Kunstinstitut, Frankfurt, Germany